BOOKS BY GUILLAUME WOLF "PROF. G"

- *You Are a Message*
- *You Are a Circle*
- *reDESIGN: reCREATE*

For information about the author, creative workshops, and additional content, please visit **www.ProfG.co**

YOU ARE A MESSAGE

MEDITATIONS FOR THE CREATIVE ENTREPRENEUR

GUILLAUME WOLF "PROF. G"

FIRST EDITION

Texts and art: Guillaume Wolf.
Copy editor: Kristin M. Jones.

Web content. *You Are a Message* comes with additional online content. This limited, complimentary offer is open to all purchasers of *You Are a Message*—to access the Web content, you must have a valid e-mail address. This offer is limited: Content and registration is subject to availability or change. By providing your e-mail address, you give the author permission to send you information on products, news, and services. In order to protect your privacy, the author does not sell, share, or trade the subscriber list with anyone for any reason. E-mail is never sent unsolicited and is only delivered to users who have provided their e-mail address in agreement to receive these e-mails. You may unsubscribe at any time. Although the offer is complimentary, the participants will be responsible for the electronic equipment needed to access the content. Neither the publisher nor the author shall be liable for any loss of profit or other commercial damages, including but not limited to special, incidental, consequential, or other damages. The terms of this offer can be changed at any time.

A portion of the proceeds from this book will be donated to charity.

For Margaux,

with all my love

THIS IS NOT REALLY A BOOK.

This is an experience, **a visual meditation on creativity and business**—just for *you*, my creative friend. This is a moment of peace, inspiration, and introspection.

This book is the follow-up to **You Are a Circle**, and this time we're going to focus together on your creative business: from finding ideas to branding and communication. All the good stuff you need to know.

This is an invitation to use both your imagination *and* your critical mind. Here, I'm not providing you with definitive answers—because no one can—but instead, I will challenge you throughout this book to question, think, and act.

Let's start right now: **Simply open the book to any page.** Find a little quote that resonates with you. Now, ask yourself these two simple questions:

1. Do I know this?

2. Am I applying this in my life and business?

You see, we all know things. The key here is to make sure to *apply* these ideas. Because, like with everything else, the power of creating only works once you apply what you know in the real world.

What you'll discover here was originally designed as a time capsule for my daughter (she's four now). Starting with the first book of the series, *You Are a Circle*, and now with *You Are a Message*, I've compiled everything I've learned over two decades as a creative consultant and artist working in various worlds: music, fashion, luxury, art, design, and youth culture. As I hinted early on, I don't know everything (no one can claim that). These short aphorisms are only meant to remind, encourage, and challenge—that's all.

This book is not for everyone, though. It's designed for the **Next Creative Class**: people like you who are changing our world for the good—not by talking about it, but by creating new offerings (businesses, organizations, and groups) based on positive creative values.

I believe in change because after years of gruesome work, trial and error, I've figured out change is not only possible, but **we can all create it**. So please know that what I'm sharing with you here is based on real-life experience, not on theory.

You see, life is a curious putty, and like a sculptor, your job is to constantly work on it—all the time. It's an ongoing practice. It's a process.

Is it easy? Nope.

Is it worth it? You bet!

Listen, **you have more power than you think**. You have in you a unique light that needs to be expressed in the world, despite countless forces around you telling you otherwise. You might start with a little, or a lot; you might start early, or late: None of this matters. It's **your resolve to act** on a project, then experiment with it until you make it work, that's going to give you the results you want.

So **today, it's your turn to shine**. It's quite simple, really. If we all decide that something needs to change, by acting together, we'll find a way to make it happen. And remember, at the very core, **change starts with you, at your own level, *right now*.**

So find what's important to you, and know why.

Then . . . go for it. Experiment. Create something new. Create something beautiful. Your life is waiting for you to shine.

Shine on, little star. Shine on.

Let your light out.

With love,
Guillaume Wolf "Prof. G"

You are a message. Everything you are, everything you have, everything you do is a message. You might not know it, but you're constantly projecting a message around you.

What's your message? What are you saying to the world around you? What are you saying to your market? What are you saying to future generations?

Don't push, pull.
To be interesting, be interested.

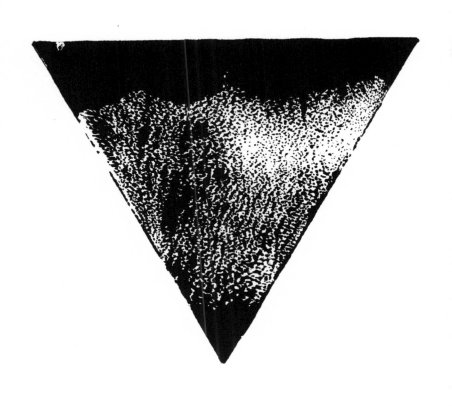

It takes guts to start a creative business.
It takes guts to follow your passion.
It takes guts to try and fail.
It takes guts to go back at it until it works.
It takes guts to live the life you want.
So, congratulations: You have guts.
Now, trust your gut.

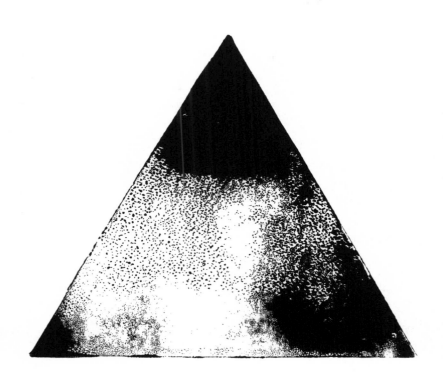

It's always about the fundamentals.
Ask yourself these two questions:

- Who am I talking to?
- How can I help them?

This is a great practice, like mental tai chi.
This is also the secret to creating a great brand.

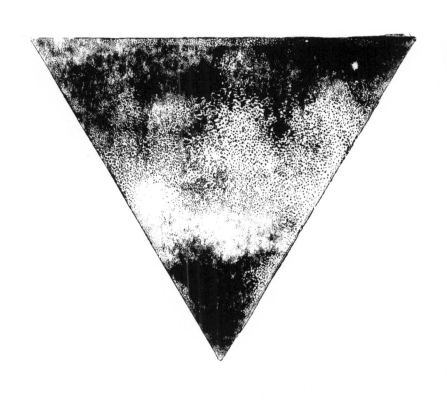

When you create your own niche, it is difficult at first.
If you succeed, you'll end up ruling your market.

In your market, do you have a unique niche?
If not, why not?

On the one hand, you have creatives/artists who are reluctant to learn marketing, fearing it might dissolve the authenticity of their message: That's called fear.

On the other hand, you have marketers who mistakenly think they can influence anyone into doing anything they want: That's called hubris.

Both are incorrect. The sweet spot is at the center: Today, you want to be a creative/artist who also knows about marketing. It's art and business; it's also business and art.

Good communication is like real magic. You can change a situation; you can make the impossible possible. It's uncanny to see it happen; it's almost spooky to realize you're behind it.

How do you train yourself? Simply start at your own level, with people around you. The next time you meet someone, try to find the gem in her, and reveal it in a sentence. But here, it's not about fake compliments. It has to be real and meaningful.

Connect with others by showing them that you see the truth and beauty that's already there. You think it sounds easy? It's not. You think it sounds cheesy? It's not. It's actually very meaningful. Now, the real question is: Are you doing it? Can you connect with others? If you've never done it, try. You'll learn a lot.

Once you've started this practice in your life, try to apply the same principle with your project. Can your brand connect with others meaningfully? How? How often?

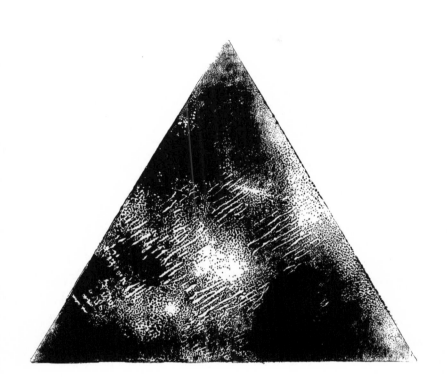

To be an effective communicator, the first thing to do is to kill your ego . . . It's not easy. But, remember, it's not about you (the creator/designer); it's about them (your audience).

How well do you know your audience?
When was the last time you hung out with them?

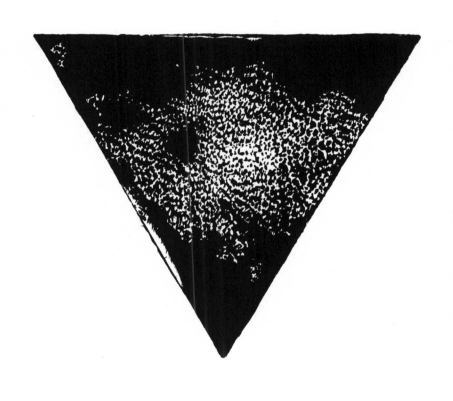

Even if they're one and the same, a company and a brand run on two different kinds of systems.

A company is a dry system where everything can be measured in numbers: production costs, distribution, sales, market shares, etc.

A brand is a wet system that exists within fuzzy concepts: cool factor, trends, desires, dreams, truths, emotions, culture, etc.

When you're in charge of a brand, you're dealing with a wet system; you're handling an ever-changing material.

Branding is a bit like surfing—you must find balance in a fluid environment.

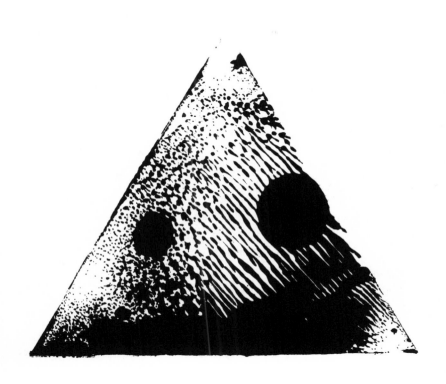

Empathy is paramount.

To understand an individual in a market, my talent is to imagine that I've flown out of my shoes and landed in his or her shoes. From this new perspective, I can see, feel, and think as he or she does. But remember, this is not a parlor trick: In order to be empathic, you need to be genuinely loving and caring.

That's what I do best, and you should try it too. By practicing empathy daily, you'll get incredible insights into people and situations.

Try this: Go to a crowded place. Look around. Pick a person completely different from you. Imagine being inside his/her body. Imagine thinking, feeling like him/her. During this exercise, come from a place of kindness (never judgment). Get a sense of how this person sees the world. Learn from it.

New luxury is time and space.
New success is the realization of your true potential.
New wealth is the cultural legacy you leave behind.
As you can see, none of these has anything to do with bling.

You can be a merchant of cool, but always be honest:
Don't you dare lie.

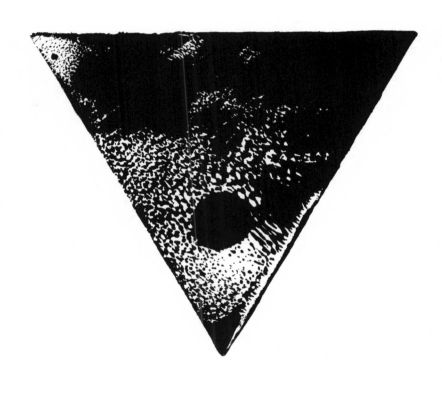

Today, everyone in the marketplace—even entry-level employ-ees—is being asked to present him- or herself as a mini-brand (with a message). A lot of creative people hate this, as they would rather have their work speak for itself. Yet denouncing "personal branding" as being a horrific trend that forces you to put on a "fake persona" is actually erroneous. Why? Simple: You can't fake this.

Your personal brand is about *your* truth. Be curious and find the truth within yourself. It can become a personal challenge to grow on a deeper level: "What do I stand for? Am I working at my full potential? Am I learning every day? Am I contributing to the world? Am I stretching myself outside of my comfort zone? Do I connect with the people who need to see what I do? In what way?"

A great person is someone who keeps evolving. Truth-based personal branding challenges you to find the resources inside you in order to grow into your best possible self.

That's a good thing.

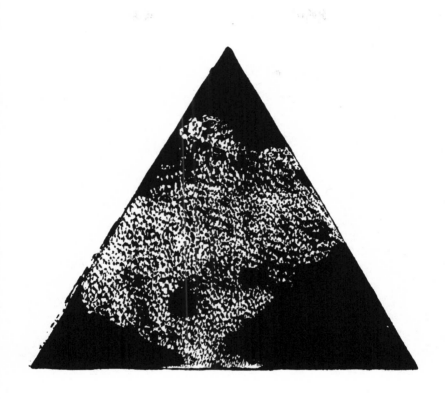

There are no extraordinary brands
without extraordinary people.
If you want to build a great brand,
challenge yourself to be the best you can be
in every area of your life, not just business.

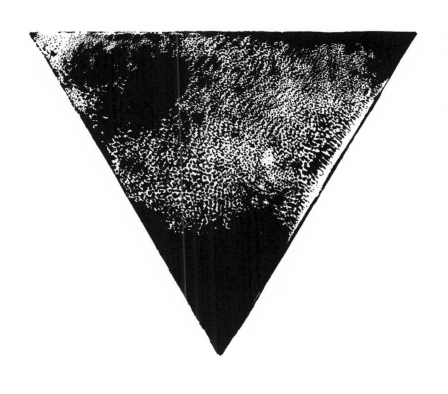

Do you matter?

This is a hard question for a person or a brand; yet, the answer is easy.

First, do something at your level that helps someone's life. Just one person.

Next, do something that impacts ten people. And keep going.

Long term, true influence is the by-product of caring for others. You'll matter the most once you start caring for the world.

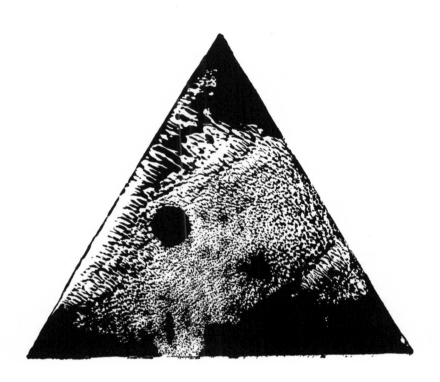

Here's the secret of failure and unhappiness: Be rigid, be self-righteous, be lazy, always look at things from a place of fear and hatred.

Here's the secret of success and happiness: Be resilient, take responsibility, work hard, always looks at things from a place of confidence and gratitude.

There are no shortcuts on this path.
Every day, short-term self-sacrifices create long-term results.

What are the daily sacrifices you must implement?
What long-term results will you get from them?

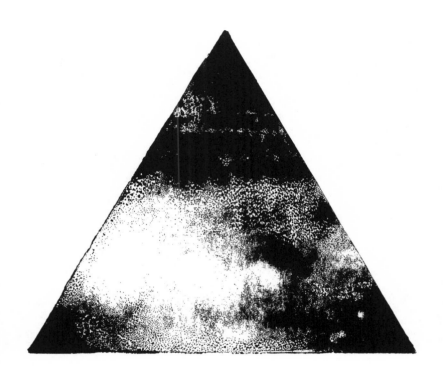

There's one force that you must combat every day. It's called the status quo: the willingness to keep things the way they are.

First, find it within yourself. Learn about it, grab it, and destroy it (Ask: What doesn't want to change within me?).

Next, be ruthless when you meet the status quo in the real world. Every time you meet someone who says, "It cannot be done," start thinking about how you're going to make it happen. That is, *without* this person around, of course.

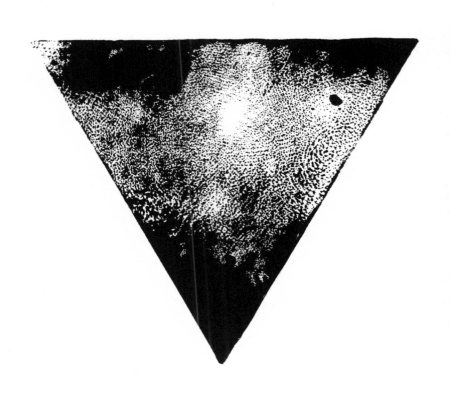

Nothing amuses me more than to see passing fads crashing on the ground. Folly is a powerful teacher that fools never learn from.

Search online for "failed marketing." It's a great (and hysterically funny) education.

Learn from the past to master the present.

As a consultant, the greatest gift you can give to a client is to uncover something that could destroy their business, and have the courage to say so. Only the very few have the nerves to do it.

Make sure you surround yourself with people who can give honest feedback, not yes-men.

Psychology is key for branding. Not clinical psychology, though. Healthy, happy psychology. Your brand must be healthy and happy.

In the past, some people treated business like guerrilla warfare, with an "anything goes" attitude.

Today, we're all interconnected and information travels fast. Know this: If you're evil (or if your brand is evil), you will be singled out and excluded, sooner or later.

We all want to hang out with the good guys, not the evildoers.

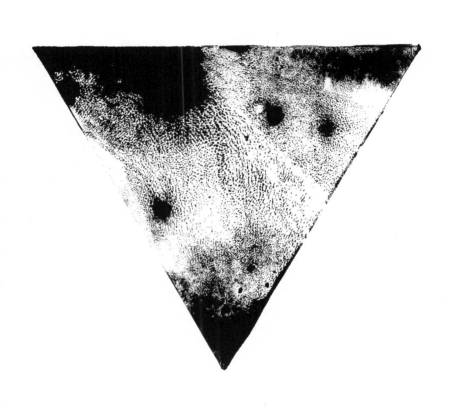

If you cultivate new talents within yourself on a regular basis, it becomes natural for you to make your brand evolve. Both are linked. Everything is always interconnected.

Once you get this, apply it with your team. Make sure that *they* always grow along with you.

What new things are you (and your team) trying this month?

To build your brand, you need three things
working simultaneously:

1. Perfect skills or products.
2. Perfect understanding of the culture you're dealing with.
3. Perfect storytelling.

Neglect one of these, and it's over.

skills/products   culture

storytelling

What's storytelling in branding?

It's every piece of communication you put out there. But there's a twist! It's also the story your customers play in *their* minds about your brand.

If you want to do great, both stories had better match.

It's great people who make a company or a brand great.
Money is not enough—you need vision and talent.

Are you surrounded by great people?

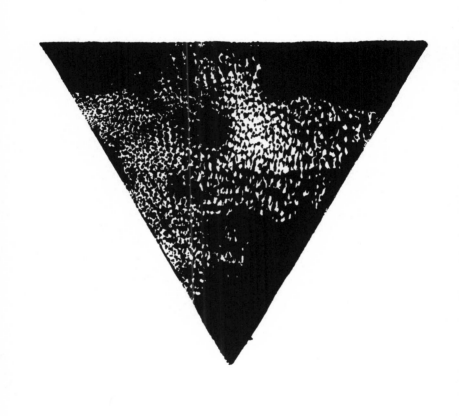

Twentieth-century communication has worked diligently to infantilize audiences. In the twenty-first century, this is a very dangerous game to play. People are not babies anymore.

How do you talk to your audience?
What's your tone?

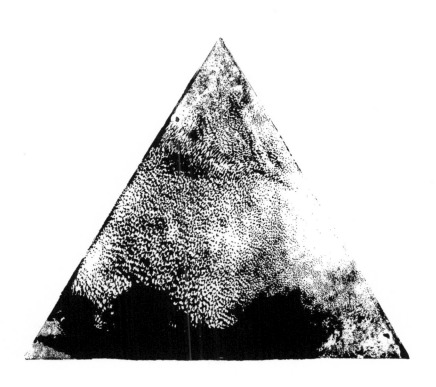

Talk to your audience as you would talk to your best friend. Be candid, be cool, be loving.

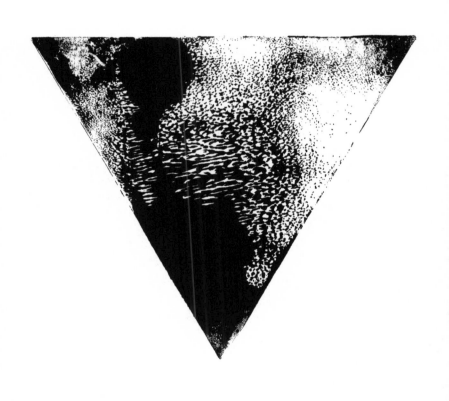

As a branding professional, you have to stand for something. You need to have values. I personally refuse to work on cigarettes, or anything that kills people. Life is already too short.

What do *you* stand for?

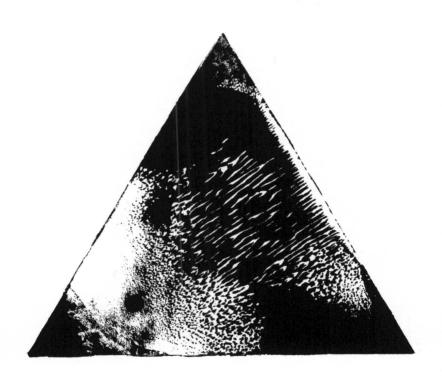

Few professionals in communication understand millennials because they don't know any. A lot of studies out there are completely wrong when it comes to youth markets. In fact, it's hilarious to see how lost these researchers are. To know youth, just get to know them. Hang out!

If your business deals with youth, in what *direct ways* do you know about them?

Brands make mistakes all the time. The smart ones say: "We're sorry we screwed up." Then, they work really hard so it never happens again.

A brand is like a person. A boring, uneducated, sexist, condescending person always ends up alone and forgotten. Same thing with a brand.

Agreed?

Try this exercise: If your brand were a person, how would a young woman describe it?

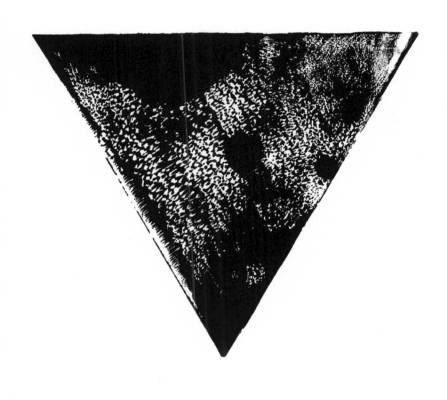

Brands desperately want to be "cool," thinking it's about following fads. This is a big mistake. Only the ones who are willing to honor their truth will collect "in-depth cool currency." The reason is simple: Nothing is cooler than the truth.

Ask yourself:
What's my brand's truth?
Does my audience understand and connect with this truth?

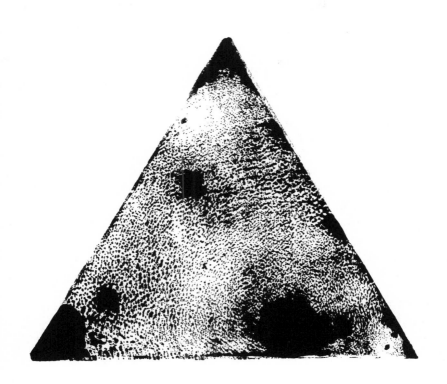

Brands and markets are living systems.
You want one to attract the other
in order to create a symbiotic relationship.

Great branding works simultaneously on attraction
and symbiosis.

You don't always need a slogan. First, let your action, your services, speak for you. Be a gentleman, and the whole world will treat you like one.

If you have one, does your slogan/motto match your action?

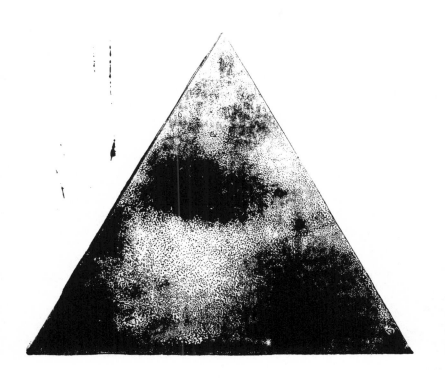

If you're weird, that might be a problem. If you're weird and smart, that might be an asset. If you're weird, smart, and understand culture, that's great.

What cool weirdness could you bring into your brand?

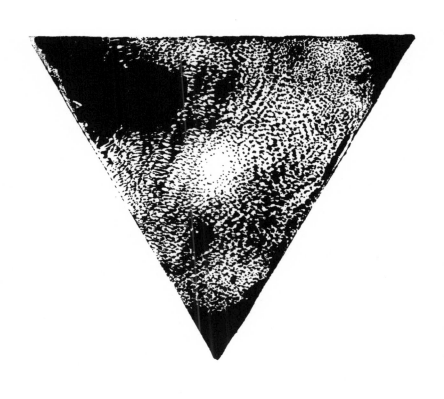

The next creative class can imagine, create, execute, negotiate, promote, and sell. This is how the game is played today.

If you're not good at one of these skills, learn it. Invest in yourself. Your education must be a lifelong process.

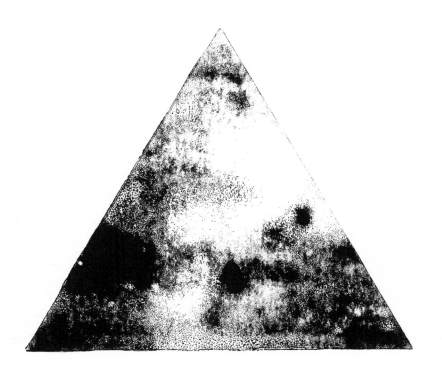

One of the greatest secrets in life is this:

If you're ready to experiment with something new, you might succeed or you might fail.

If you succeed, good for you. If you fail (and if you survive), all is not lost. You have a chance to look at things really clearly. You have a chance to learn something and try again with a different approach. It might be horrible and you will be forced to change. That's a good thing. Keep at it and try again. If you do, life has a deal in store for you: She will make you stronger.

Fail the right way and something is given to you. That's the deal with life.

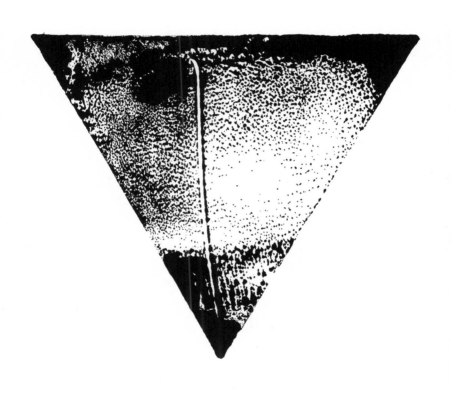

The person or company with a larger wallet is not smarter than you, just more comfortable.

This is great news for the little ones. Comfort is the enemy of innovation.

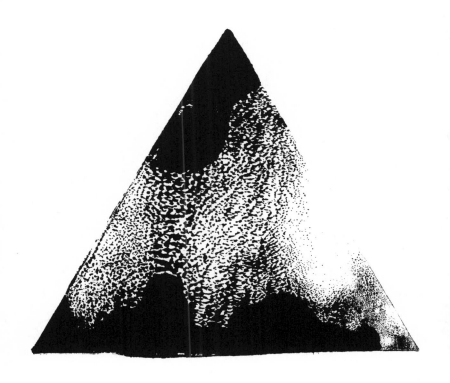

The next level is about moving from "me" to "we." If we win together, our compounded success will bring untold rewards. That's why successful rappers have a posse. When one artist gets picked up, the rest will follow. So get your posse in place; partner with others.

But watch out—make sure everyone understands the concept first.

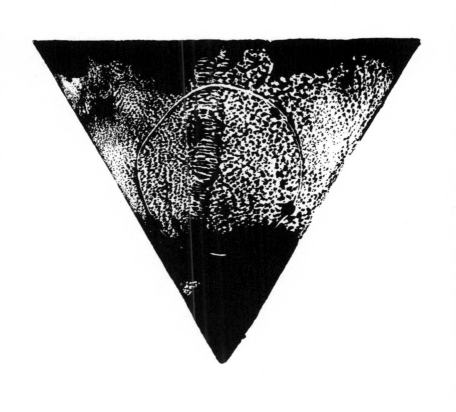

Do you remember the tale of the tortoise and the hare?

The tortoise and the hare agree to do a race. The hare, who's naturally gifted, doesn't take the race seriously. The tortoise does and arrives on time. The race starts, and the tortoise gets going, one step at a time. But the hare, who looks down on the tortoise, decides instead to eat first, then rest . . . and gets completely distracted. Time passes. Suddenly, the hare sees the tortoise getting closer to the finish line. He rushes in, trying to catch up . . . but it's too late. The tortoise wins.

This children's story is very powerful because it talks about one of the most important talents you can cultivate in your life: focus.

Your focus is the secret engine that drives all your actions. It's the compass that will bring you back to your goals, regardless of the circumstances you might face.

Focus supports you in achieving real, valuable goals: goals that may take ten, twenty, or thirty years to achieve. Focus is the force behind mastery. Focus allows you to pulverize incredible obstacles. Focus is a secret ally that allows you to defy both time *and* probabilities.

Yes, you might be discouraged; you might even lose your enthusiasm for a while . . . but if you still have your focus, you will find a way. You will succeed.

Be like the tortoise. *Focus.*

focus

Are you a computer, a Sim™, or a robot?
I hope not.

We are taught since childhood to think in binary mode:
Yes/no, right/wrong, win/lose, etc.

This view of the world is reinforced everywhere as we grow up. From education to popular culture, we are being presented with a binary world: "This is the right way, this is the wrong way." In social interactions, we are also expected to act in a binary mode (like a computer, a Sim™, or a robot).

Unfortunately, this mental map of the world is completely obsolete. It only works short term.

In business, binary thinking blocks innovation.

In personal life, it's a sure way to unhappiness.

Instead, a new way to approach any problem is to think trinary. How does it work?

Simply start in binary mode: First, find the two opposites. Next, create a strange hybrid of both. Next, imagine the opposite of that. Keep pushing yourself; challenge yourself intellectually. Explore.

Imagine something never seen before, something that's all inclusive. Imagine something outside of the mental map everyone else is using. Consider the opposite of what the herd is doing. Try thinking like someone else (see p. 28).

It takes some time to learn operating in trinary mode, but that's how you will come up with disruptive ideas and innovate. At the core, all living systems are trinary, not binary. Trinary thinking is a model that allows you to navigate living systems effectively. By using it, you will come up with incredible ideas.

Ask yourself: What's the third perspective here?

1   2

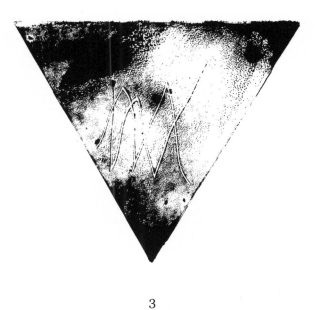

3

Think trinary: 3 *is* the magic number.

I love to be surrounded by smart people. Their oozing brain cells make me a bit smarter too. I can see the world from their perspective, and that's refreshing. I don't just listen, I step inside their reality. Try it—it's fun.

If you say to yourself, "But I have no time!" ask yourself how much TV you watch per week. I have all the time in the world, because I don't own a TV.

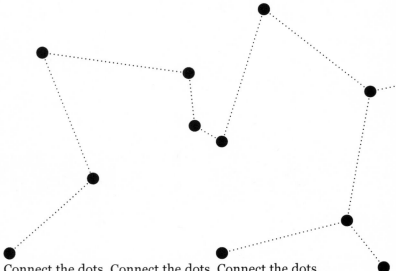

Connect the dots. Connect the dots. Connect the dots.
Everything is in front of you, right now. Make new connections
with what you already have. How? Introduce people who don't
know each other. Imagine combining different activities into
one. Play a bit with what you think is your reality. *Hack it.*

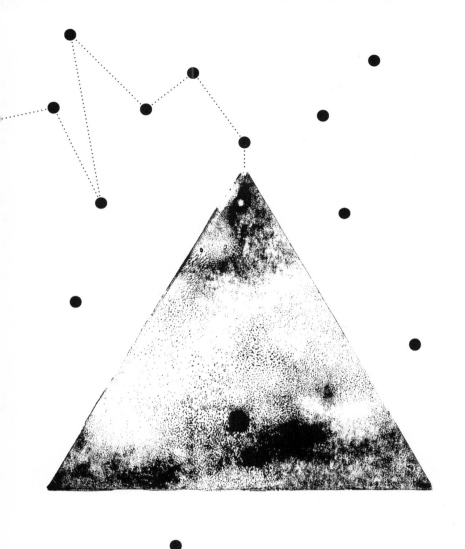

Where can I grow?
Where can I improve?
What should I try next?

These are amazing questions to ask yourself daily, when you have the willingness to act on them.

Be a learner all your life.
The second you think you're a genius, you're a has-been.

Work hard. Work really hard. But be gentle with yourself at the end of each day. Review what you did. Look at your actions. Did you do your best today? Good. Now you can sleep tight. You did a good job.

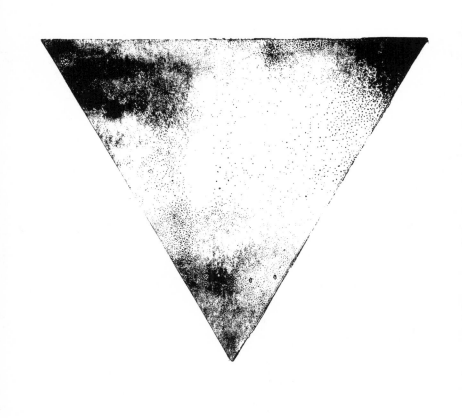

You can't control people.
You can't control reality.
You can't control your market.

But . . .

You can connect with people.
You can connect with reality.
You can connect with your market.

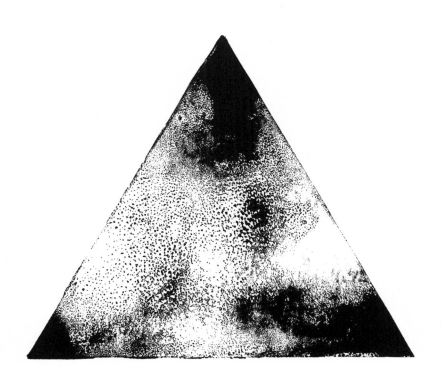

Leadership is always taken, never given. Anyone can become a leader—it has nothing to do with your title. You can be a leader, today, the moment you start acting like one.

The next time there's a major problem at work, step up: Be the one who creates a solution.

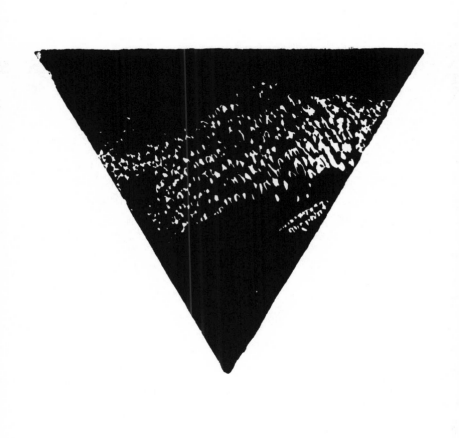

At some point in your life, you might negotiate a contract with a corporate lawyer gone rogue. Don't be intimidated. Have her change anything you don't like. It doesn't matter how long it will take. You should never sign a deal that contains one line that might work against you in the future.

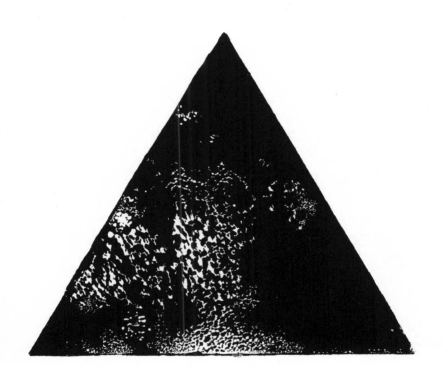

What's your greatest currency? It's:

How you are perceived in your market.
How much they love you.

Do you want your customers to love you? First, ask yourself:
In what ways are you showing them your love?

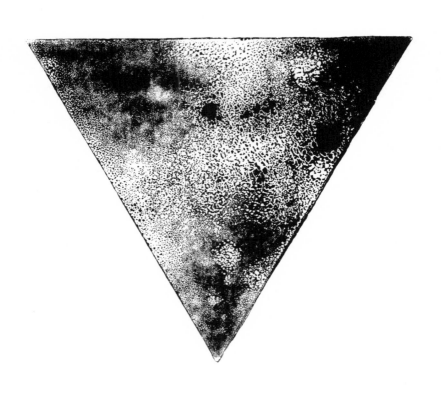

It's not just what you do, it's how you share the story of what you do. All the greatest are master storytellers. If you don't know how to tell a story about yourself and your brand, you can learn this skill. How? Watch Steve Jobs or Philippe Starck do a live presentation. Get a pen and write down what they're saying. See how they've built their story. Storytelling is an all-powerful force.

Having a big vision for yourself and your brand is important. But instead of just thinking about numbers, try thinking about how you can change people's lives.

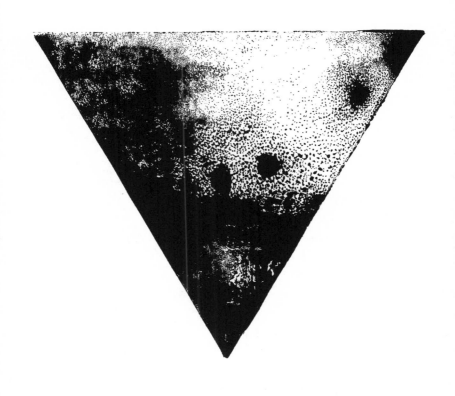

Design done well is magical. But it's not enough.

People still get excited when they learn I did the Colette logo.*
Personally, I get excited remembering how hardworking, caring, and culturally savvy the founders were. It's easy to be mes-
merized by hype instead of looking at the hard work and ethics
behind any success.

* Parisian fashion superstore,
described by the *New York Times* as
"the coolest store in town."

If you think you need a lucky break to succeed, something is not quite right and you need to fix it. It's never about luck. If you're the absolute best at what you do, success comes to you. That's how it works.

If you know you're not good enough in your niche, either perfect yourself until you become the best, or move to a slightly different niche. Choose battles where you have an edge, even an offbeat edge . . . have something others don't.

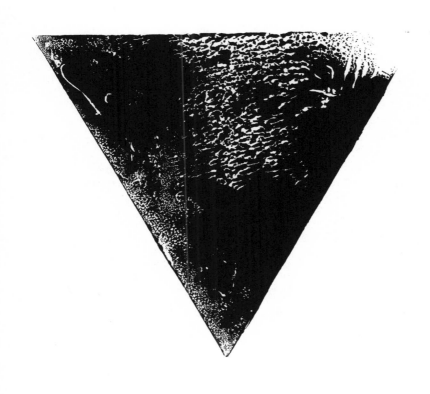

All the creatives I know are multitalented, and this is danger-ous. Sure, it's fun to play; but after you're done experimenting you'll have to focus on one thing. Out of everything you can do, what is by far the one thing that makes you completely unique? What were you born to do? Focus on that for work. Keep doing the other stuff for fun.

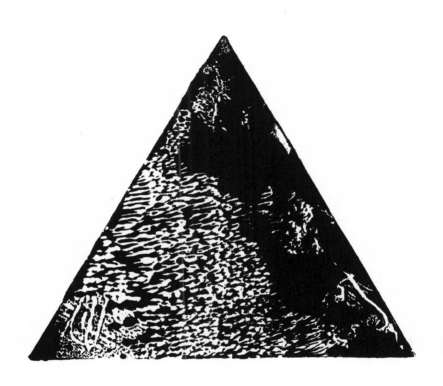

Great branding is almost identical to dating. When it's done right, it's about creating a meaningful connection. It's never about cheesy pickup lines.

It's true that we all have enormous potential.
It's true that it takes a lot of courage and extreme hard work
to bring that potential forward.
It's true that in the process, you will get hurt a lot.
It's all true, and it's all worth it.

There's a new breed of creatives out there who have an interesting view of life: They get the idea of whole, interconnected, living systems.

If you're one of them, keep making these connections. Keep mapping new territories. Good things are coming your way.

We all live as different parts of one unified living system. You and I are not separate. This is the most beautiful realization, when you finally get it.

If this idea is new for you, keep at it: This insight and mental map will support you in creating change and long-term, sustainable growth, both in your life and in your business.

What whole, living system are you a part of?
Do you know every corner of that system?
How can you move beyond the limits of that system?

How do you build an awesome team? The most magical thing I know is this: If you find the good in people and you acknowledge it . . . behold! They become good. You might need to dig deep sometimes, but it's always worth it.

How do you acknowledge the good in the people around you? How often do you celebrate it?

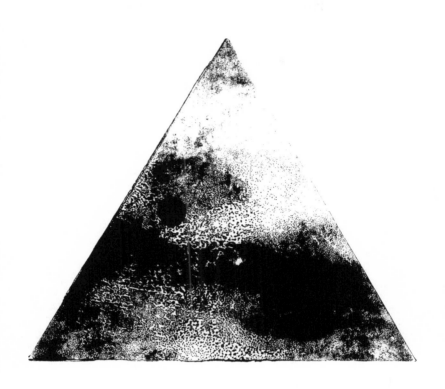

Gratitude at the end of the day.
No matter what.
Always.

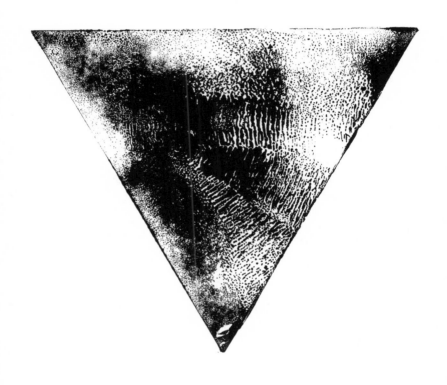

What you can do alone is limited.
Build with others.
Share with others.
Become an unlimited force.

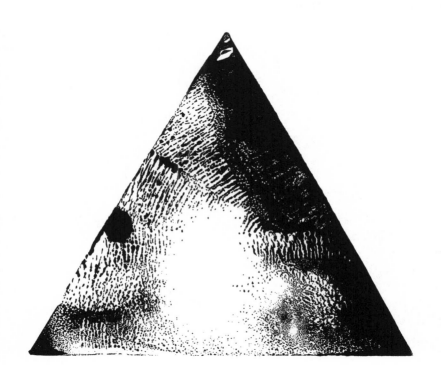

Think meta—look at the big picture. If you do, you'll find out that life is a mystery, and you'll be happy to be a part of it. You'll be happy to work within it.

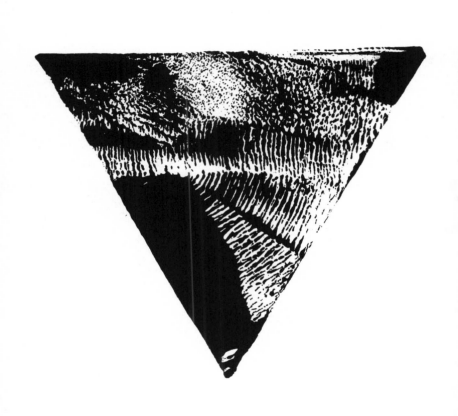

The people who have influenced my thinking the most are Buckminster Fuller, Joseph Campbell, Carl Jung, David Bohm, and Brion Gysin. If you don't know who they are, please do yourself a favor and check them out.

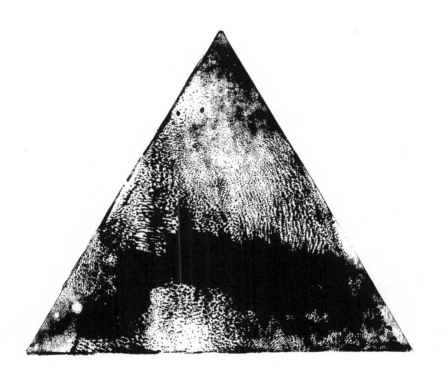

Old-school, hardcore marketers are like black magicians. They create fear, they use fear, they sell fear. There's one catch, though: They also die in fear.

In your marketing, always refuse to use fear. Instead, use love and growth. You'll not only stand out and be more successful, you'll also live a good life.

If you're interested in branding and communication, try working with a small nonprofit once in a while.

Why?

This is the hardest challenge of all. But if you figure it out, you'll take your skills to the next level. And here, I'm talking about *massive* growth. You'll gain from it, and you'll help people in need—how cool is that?

The more you help others, the more you help yourself.

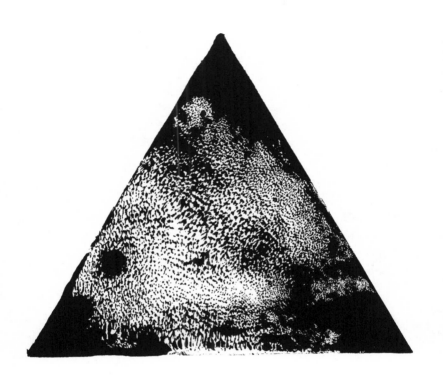

Popular culture always presents us with role models that are big-mouthed extroverts. The few geniuses I have ever met were never like that. Introverts who are willing to work hard to open up are the most powerful bunch.

Are you a smart introvert?
Here's my challenge:
Sign up for a public speaking class.
Sign up for a dance class.
Do it! You'll thank me later.

Watch out when using planned obsolescence—your market may understand very well what you're doing. People talk. If you sell crap, *you* will become obsolete.

Start with your passion, not just the cash that you think you're going to make. I promise that if you dedicate your entire life to doing things you hate, you may get rich, but you'll end up being this bitter guy, locked up in his mansion with a drink in his hand, wondering, "What if?" Believe me, I've seen these sad souls more than I care to count.

To live longer, and happier, start with your passion. And don't you dare tell me it's too late to try. As long as you have a pulse, you're good to go. One day of doing good is worth one hundred meaningless days.

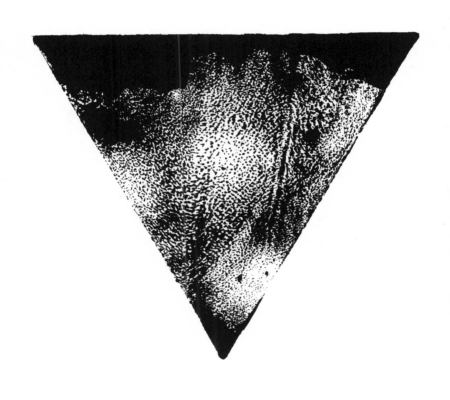

When it comes to branding, watch out for slogans that can place a negative idea in the minds of your customers.

For example, "Stay afloat" may sound cool and adventurous, but it also suggests that your brand or your clients are slowly sinking. Not good.

Understand that slogans work like spells. Only use the ones that are completely life-affirming. Remember, people connect with your brand to get inspired . . . positively inspired!

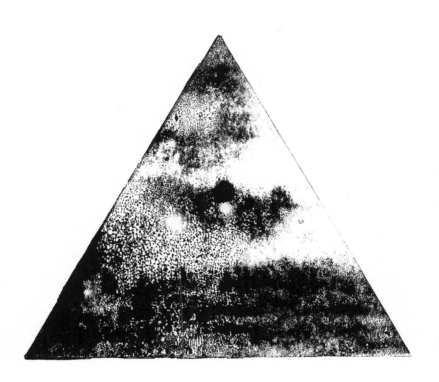

We are the by-product of the cultural living system we're a part of. We make our decisions based on what our peers like, feel, and think. Scary, isn't it?

Not so much. All you have to do is make sure you're surrounded by good people and a good environment.

If you're not, go find them.

What's a good environment or living system? It's a place where all the parties involved have access to meaningful growth.

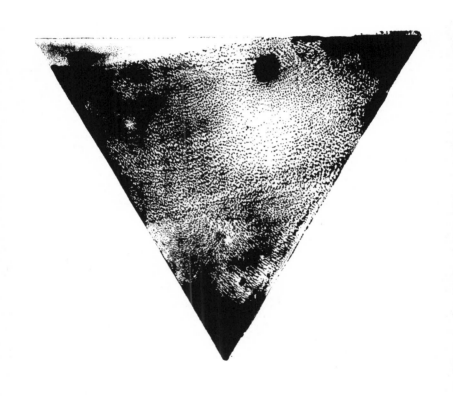

The best way to assess a brand culture and find out if it's attractive is to simply ask yourself:

Would I pass on this culture to my child?

Pattern recognition is an awesome skill to have, only if you're simultaneously open to discovering the maverick element* that will disturb the pattern.

Change in any industry is never incremental; it's disruptive.

Ask yourself: How can I bring something completely new into my market? How would it look if I were to do the opposite of what everyone else is doing?

* If you haven't already, please read *The Black Swan,* by Nassim Nicholas Taleb.

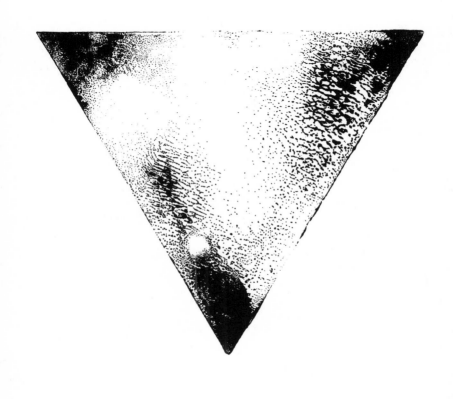

You can study, survey, and analyze your market until the end of times . . . but do you understand it? Do you have a *feel* for it? If you don't, find someone that does.

If you want to understand love, don't ask a laboratory technician to tell you about the chemistry of dopamine, oxytocin, and vasopressin. Instead, find an artist who knows about love.

If you want to understand cool, same thing: Find an artist who knows about cool. Everything that's elusive in our human experience calls for art, not for science. In these realms, the artist is always stronger than the researcher.

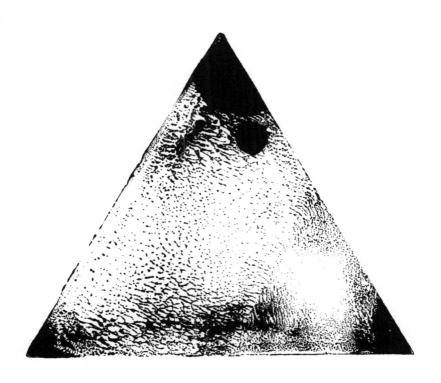

There's this thing called living by inspiration. It's better than living by desperation. Make sure your brand is always inspired, *and* inspiring.

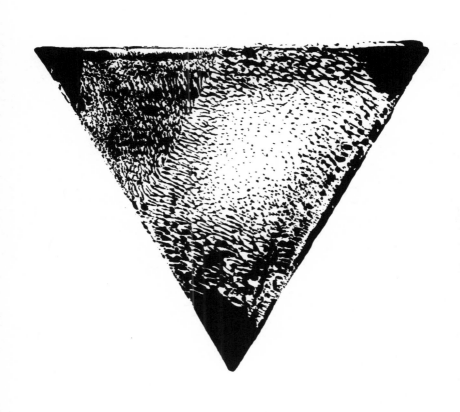

Don't let clients tell you they have "just a little budget" for you. If this happens, it can mean three things:

• You're not good enough and you need to improve.
• They're playing you, and you should not work with them.
• You're great, but they don't know about it, and you should educate them on the value you provide.

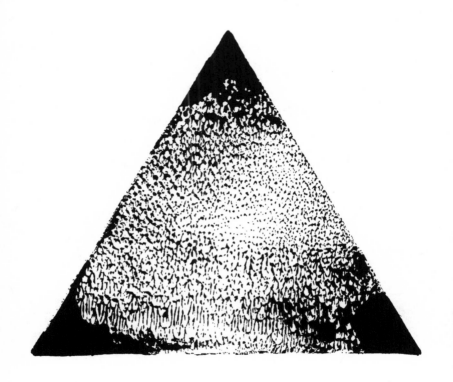

Every day, you'll have to take calculated risks in order to get unexpected results. The amazing isn't manifested by the banal.

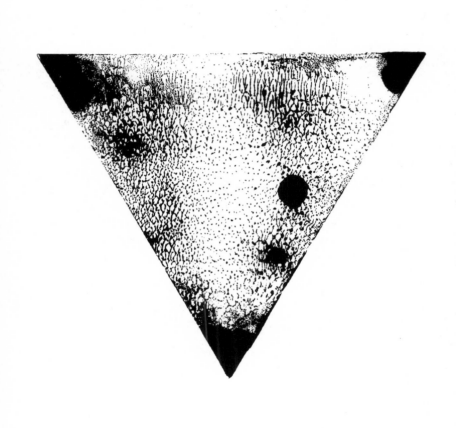

Even if you're just a guy selling T-shirts,* imagine selling them in different countries. Would they sell in Tokyo? In what store, do you think? Look it up . . . Find their address, contact them, and show them your goods. See what happens. Keep doing this kind of stuff, and soon you'll have supporters in every country.

* In this story, your T-shirts must be seriously amazing. That's a given. Whatever you sell, it needs to be great—it needs to be a part of a unique story.

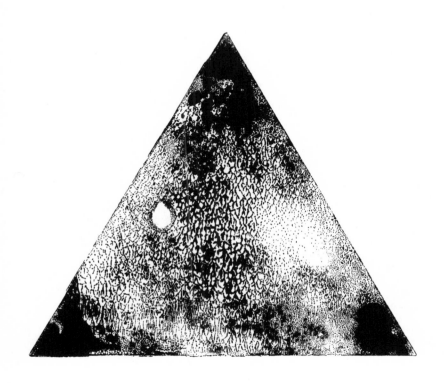

If you're really down, if nothing works for you, if you can't take it anymore and want to end it all—don't.

Go to bed, and wait one more day. Then try again, change your approach a bit. Every day, refine your gesture . . .

If you keep at it and you keep growing and adapting, something will work.* I promise.

* Start reading about the lives of world leaders throughout history. You will be surprised. All of them surmounted incredible obstacles, and so can you. We human beings are built to adapt.

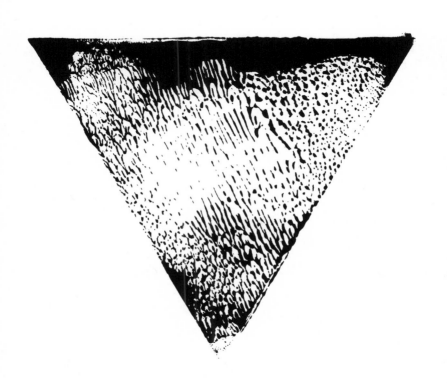

In branding or in life, when you tell the truth, people take you seriously. When you tell the truth, and you make a positive impact, they'll start trusting you. And if you honor that trust by always delivering on your promises, they'll stay close to you for a very long time.

This the right way to navigate through life, and this is the right way to build a solid brand.

Never dumb down what you want to do, but make sure you talk about it the right way. Learn to share what you do with others effectively.

How? Here's a tip: Simply tell them *why* you love it so much. Share your passion. Let your enthusiasm roar.

If you're a chocolate maker, after hearing you talk, I should want to have chocolate for dinner, every day, for the rest of my life.*

* Mast Brothers, I love you. Keep up the good work.

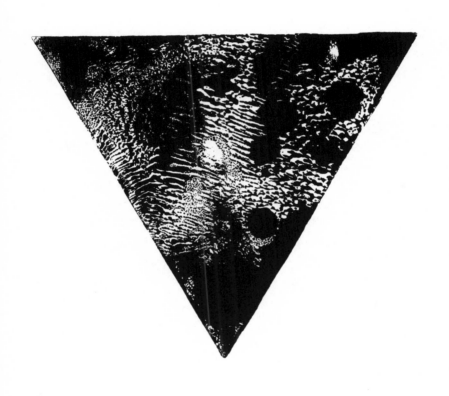

It's funny that we use this term "brand identity." Identity is such a complex subject in human life.

When you think about a brand identity, you need to look beyond a logo, design, and typeface choices. You must realize that you're creating an entity with a personality.

It's interesting to think about it the same way that a fiction writer does when creating a character. Your brand should have opinions, feelings, and goals; just like a good character in a story.

Meet your two new best friends.
These are two questions:

- What if this could be done?
- What would this look like?

These are the kind of questions that force you to think in the right direction. These questions *are* your friends.

To create a quantum shift in your business, you should focus on developing the attraction factor of your brand.

- Are you the hottest thing around in your market?
- Do you have cult status?

You must answer yes to both of these. If not, work at it. You simply can't survive by being just average.

So you ask, "How do I make my brand attractive?" You must perfect what I call your "O.K.S."

It's three things combined:

> • Your Offering (product, experience, or skills)
> +
> • Your Knowledge of culture (past and present, and future forecast)
> +
> • Your Storytelling (your brand philosophy, and how it's delivered)

While "O.K.S." sounds cute, it's really hard to get it right. The difficulty is that these elements cannot be static—they must constantly evolve over time.

Rebranding is a bit like doing a makeover. It's completely useless if not backed up by a real, inner change. No matter how hard you try, a new logo can't change a rotten culture. So before you rebrand, make sure your culture is correct.

What's a correct culture? It's an environment where everyone involved (your team and customers) are delighted to participate in your brand. Once you get that right, everything else follows.

You ask, "What's being current with the times?"

Today, it's about taking a stand for what's fair. It's about cross-cultural pollination and friendship.

Don't trust mainstream media to tell you what's up—they don't have a clue. Observe growing niche markets and learn from them instead. The gem always lies in the positive wave of change that makes our culture evolve.

You are not just selling a product, a service, or an experience. You are creating a world, a space of freedom for others.

Your job is to make your world so amazing that everyone in your market wants to be a part of it.

There are brands that have so much negativity around them, they can't be saved. No one can turn them around. And when it happens, it's entirely their fault.

Make sure you listen to your customers. If you hear the same complaint twice: Fix it as if your life depends on it.

Your customers are not morons. They know exactly when you try to con them with a bad deal or product.

Only offer them something that you would offer to a loved one.

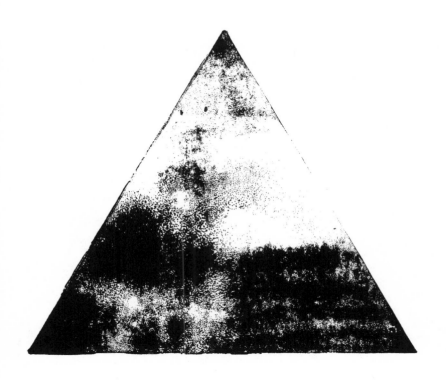

There's a major shift coming up. A lot of very large companies are going to fail in the coming decades. Why? They poison either the environment or their customers. When you kill people and/or the planet, we all notice.

Don't hire a PR firm to spin your image in a good way; you would waste your time. You can't fake an image today. Instead, save your money, and work hard to do good.

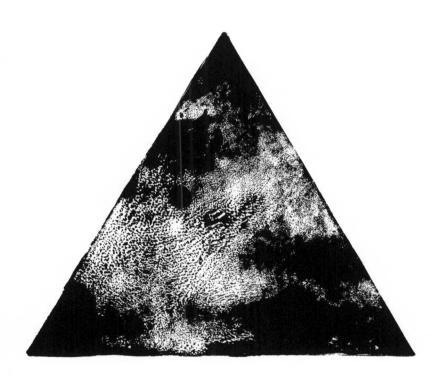

How do you create an irresistible brand? Offer your market something irresistible. Today, being irresistible is not about being cheap, it's about being true.

Solve a tiny problem for me and I'll give you five dollars. Solve a bigger problem for me and I'll give you a hundred dollars. Make me a grow as an individual while you help me solve my problem, and I will be your customer for life.

Try avoiding using chemicals that make people sick (or that kill rodents in labs). We all can read labels. And yes, we also can tell our children, "This is poison!" Never forget: Brand priming always starts at home.

Once you understand that life is about change, embrace it.
Become an agent of change, always.
Change is intimidating, yet it's immensely attractive.

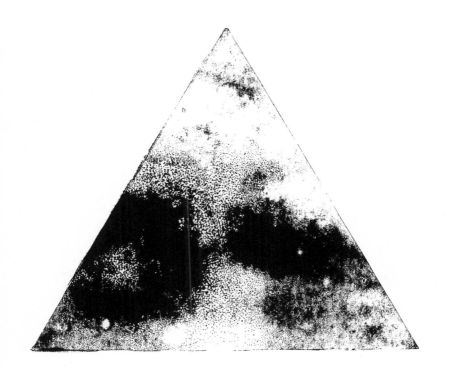

Look at trends, and always ask yourself:
What's the opposite of that?
You might come up with very interesting ideas.

While bad taste stills abounds, good taste is growing world-wide. It's incredible, but true.

I spend a lot of time looking at random social media profiles from people all around the world, and it's very clear: There's a growing global agreement on what looks good, within each market. Style *is* important.

A lot of big brands still have no clue about this. It's both shocking and hilarious.

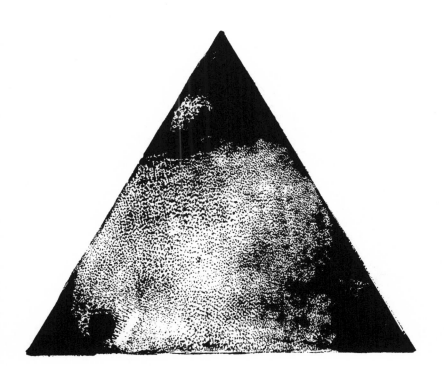

If you think you know youth culture, but you're not surrounded by youth, you don't know squat.

Today, the real value is in critical thinkers who not only can recognize patterns, but are daring enough to come up with disruptive strategies to bend them. Ideally, you should have someone like that in every company. The catch is that they're rarer than gold.

In what ways are you encouraging your team to exercise their critical-thinking muscles?

As a creative entrepreneur, you might be tempted to do everything alone. Can you, really? Can you do everything perfectly well? Make sure that you identify your weak spots and hire a team to help you with whatever task you can't do well. This will save you time, and your sanity.

What's the first area where you need to hire help?
What's the next one?

Creativity arises from the friction
and synthesis of opposites. Play with them.

• Combine two trends that should not be together.
• Take two business models with different streams of
revenue. Next, imagine creating a new, hybrid version.
• Try going analog, if your work is digital.
• Try going digital, if your work is analog.
• Take something old and new, and mix them together.
• Take something fast, and make it slow.
• Take something cheap, and turn it into something of value.*
• Enter a category where you're not expected.
• Compress time: Challenge yourself and complete a project
in just one week.
• Play with sizes, shapes, and textures.
• Share your unique, local experience worldwide.
• Make your standardized product feel unique.
• Ask children to brainstorm with you on your complex
projects—let them go nuts. See what they come up with.

Don't be scared to explore weird ideas. No matter what, keep
playing with opposites. Find that third option!

*Starbucks' tour de force.

To disrupt a market, you have to be a contrarian.
To be a contrarian, question everything you see.

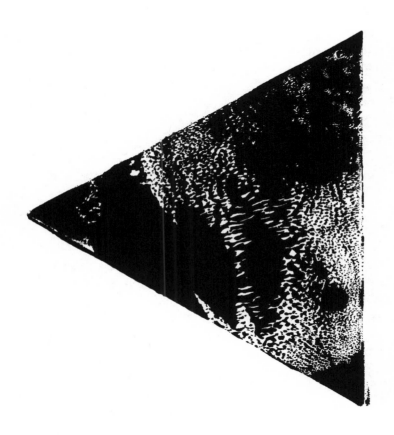

The best training is to be curious about the world around you. Look at every marketing/branding piece you see, from a cereal box to a car company's billboard. Ask yourself: Who are they talking to? What's their message? Does it feel right? Is it modern? What are the alternatives? How would I do it?

And, if you have kids, ask them what they think too. They'll see details that might elude you.

Do this for a few years, and you'll get incredible insights on branding. This type of ongoing analysis is a secret weapon. All great communicators do it.

Starting at around age ten, I was very lucky to be trained by an ad man* (my best friend's dad) to decipher branding and ad campaigns. This was the most valuable training I've ever received because it became a lifelong habit.

Looking to understand the reasoning behind every message you see is both fascinating and illuminating. Why? After a while, you start understanding how ideas work in our society, and it prompts you to do better.

* Thank you, Denis Bonnet (Ogilvy One). You were a good man and a great mentor.

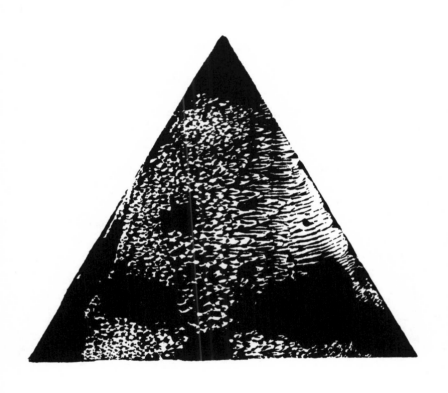

Test everything, but don't do it yourself. Pick people from your audience and have them experience what you have to offer. Watch them, as if you were not there. If they struggle with something, don't intervene—keep watching. Next, go back to the drawing board until you get it right.

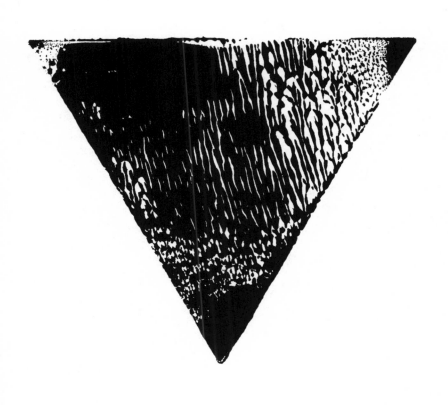

The beloved American genius Buckminster Fuller had a rough start. Unemployed after failing with a business he had started, he was contemplating suicide. Yet, prompted by the sudden insight that he had no right to end his own life, he decided to shift his work and his life into a new direction: an experiment in individual initiative. Calling himself "Guinea Pig B," he went on dedicating his energy to solving humanity's problems (instead of trying to be successful just for himself) . . .

Think about this story for a long time.

      If your life were an experiment, in what way could you be helping others? How would you contribute to the greater good by using your talent?

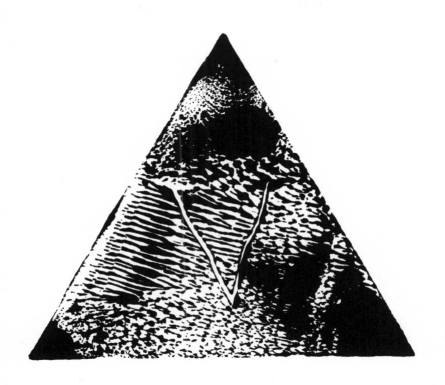

Here's the funny thing: If you only listen to others, you will be incited to be part of what's happening *right now*. Sounds good, at first. Yet, before you jump in, make sure you're the right fit for "it." If you're just following a business/creative trend, you might very likely end up becoming a follower.

Not good.

You want to lead. You want to march to the beat of your own drum and offer something unexpected.

To be great, be different.

What if brands bought wastelands and planted magnificent forests instead? Would this work?

Let's see . . .

Everyone loves a beautiful forest. Everyone loves a hero brand.

If you're a CEO and you want to impress the world, use a tiny bit of your marketing budget to try this idea out. See what happens.

No matter what you'll end up doing, know that the future belongs to heroes. Be one of them.

There are so many fears that can plague creatives and lead them to paralysis. Yet when you really look into it, you will find out that all of these fears relate to this thing we call identity.

It's a form of twisted movement that attacks the self. "If I fail with this; then I will be no good," "If I try this; then they're going to mock me," etc.

The only way out is to take your "identity" with a grain of salt. It's not about you, it's just about doing an experiment.
At some point you might fail at something. And your job is to say to yourself: "Wow, that experiment did not go too well. Now, how do I get back on that horse?"

When you treat everything as an experiment, you're naturally willing to try, and try again—for as long as you need. "Failing" doesn't mean you're not good. It means you were courageous enough to try tackling something hard in the first place. It means that you're a courageous individual. And *that* daring spirit should define your identity.

The biggest challenges always hide the greatest opportunities. This is a very important moment in human history because, collectively, we've realized that we have a lot on our hands. It's a turning point.

This is the moment where we can decide together to do good. And it starts with you. Right now. The world needs your greatness. Step aside for a second and let it out. Go for it.

Here's a little mind experiment I'd like you to try.

Sometimes we look at dated photographs from the seventies and we say: "What were they thinking?" Now imagine you are looking at the present moment from a future perspective, and ask, "What were they thinking?" Identify what needs to be changed today, and make it your job to change it.

If you do, you will rule the future.

Your greatest asset is your capacity to dream about something great, and implement it while everyone else is still asleep.

Naming your brand is a tricky business because names have a subconscious appeal. That's why actors and artists change their names. Words have a mysterious power that transcends reason.

When you name your brand, product, or service, make sure it's open-ended enough to allow a space for dreaming. Your name should reflect the spirit of what you're about. It should be inspiring, not just descriptive.

If everyone tells you to use a supermodel for your brand because everyone is using supermodels, don't. Instead, you can surprise and disrupt your market by using something completely different, such as an illustration, or a "real" person. But watch out—you need to find the right angle, the right story. If you do it correctly, it works to be different.

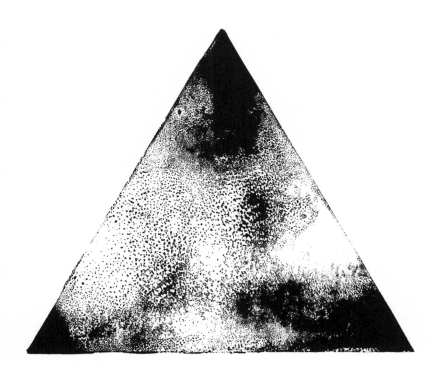

A little branding trick is to review all the senses when you think about your brand: visual, audio, tactile, and olfactory.

Real estate agents know this: The smell of fresh-baked cookies will create an instant emotional connection while people are visiting a home for sale. But as always, there are no shortcuts: A horrible artificial home freshener is not a substitute for the cookie smell.

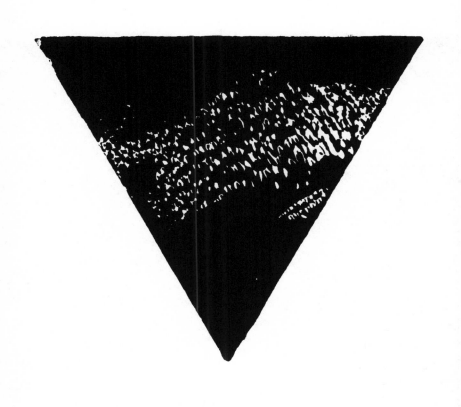

The goal for you and your brand is to reach world-class level at something. It can be anything. Just be the best in the world at it. Nothing less is acceptable.

Once you have become the best in the world, challenge yourself to improve every day.

There's a class of marketers whose only goal is to create "magic bullet" products and offerings. Interestingly, they only appeal to the feeble-minded, the gullible, and the very tired. Through infomercials, mainstream TV has provided us with millions of these gadgets, and now we see the same crap on the Web.

For your own sake, stay out of that game. It's a dark world with a lot of bad karma. Instead of "magic solutions," can you offer something real?

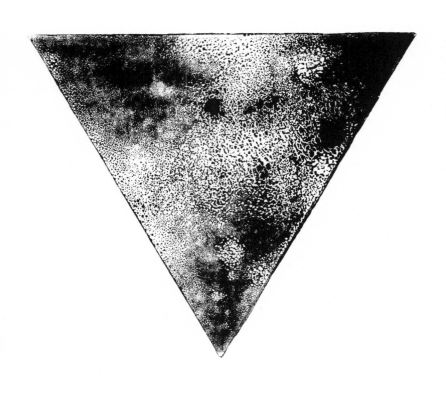

These are the days of the designers. If you have the right designers working with you, you will outmatch the competition. Apple would not be Apple without Jonathan Ive. One person with superior skills and a superior vision can indeed make a difference.

A solid culture of design is primordial in today's landscape. But it's not just the culture, it's the *people* that make that culture.

According to the Renaissance philosopher (and maverick) Giordano Bruno, desire is the most powerful force in the universe. This is true.

When your desire is perfectly aligned with the desire of your audience or market, success is just a question of time.

Start with them first. What are they looking for, right now? What's their most pressing desire?

Know their core desire. Help them fulfill it. But please, also make sure that in the process they become great and happy. Help them morph into their best possible self.

Your market is asking you:

- Can you create a world that I want to become a part of?
- Can you create a brand that I want to support?
- Can you create stories that inspire me?

Your market is asking you great questions. Are you listening?

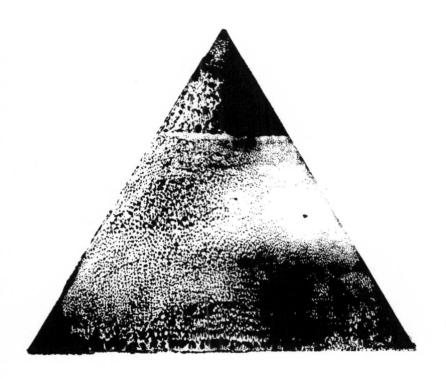

Great branding and communication are not really like psychotherapy, but more akin to shamanism.

The greatest influencers of our times are all modern shamans. You don't believe me? Look up "Steve Jobs + reality distortion field." You'll be surprised.

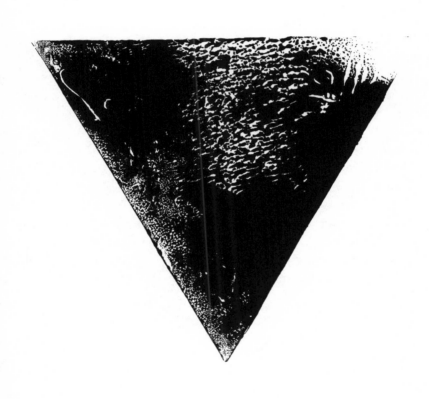

You must be a translator and connector of ideas and cultures.
You must be a translator and connector of ideas and cultures.
You must be a translator and connector of ideas and cultures.

Yes, I just wrote this three times.
Why?
Well, it's great when you get it.
But . . . it's (take a deep breath) *EarthShattering-OMG-You'reAGenius-HotThingYou-WeLoveYouSoMuch-AwesomePossum-CrystalMagicSuperpowers-CosmicRaysForces-UnicornsAreReal-SayWhat?-ChampagneAndCaviarForBreakfast-KoalaMilkBath-DidThisJustHappen?-YesItDid-PlanetaryHappinessForAll* . . .
all of this *and* much more . . . *when (and only when)* <u>you apply it.</u>

In the coming years, I feel we might continue to see dramatic changes in the ways people interact with brands.

First, there was the practice of co-creation: users spontaneously telling brands what they want, what kind of brand culture and values they expect. This type of instant feedback loop mechanism is very impressive in itself.

The next step is co-participation: disruptive brands asking users to create the experience with other users: eBay, Wikipedia, Airbnb, Uber, Lyft, etc., using real-time reviews and feedback to filter out potential "bad seeds."

It's obvious: There's a movement toward getting closer. But what's the next level? Symbiotic wholeness? What would this look like?

Curiously, the study of other life forms could give us a clue. In the incredible book *The Superorganism*,* we learn that in insect societies, intelligence is the by-product of all the individuals involved, functioning together as one whole—what you could imagine as being one "intelligent operating wholeness."

Could this be a next step into brand creation and human evolution? We shall see. But no matter what, things are changing—we're getting closer to one another.

The Superorganism, by Bert Hölldobler and E. O. Wilson.

Talking about my previous book, *You Are a Circle*,* one reviewer called me "naive." Which is fine (you can call me whatever you want). But there's a catch—it's also completely (and hilariously) inaccurate.

In fact, I'm possibly the least naive person you'll ever meet. For me, ignorance is not bliss. It's a freaking nightmare.

So if you ever hear me talk about something daring, I'm simply being enthusiastic. Why? Because your enthusiasm is the force that bends reality. Your enthusiasm is the power that prompts you to take the lead when everyone else has given up. Your enthusiasm will move people and situations. Your enthusiasm will help you achieve what everyone else said was impossible.

In my experience, there's nothing naive about that. Enthusiasm is a powerful force. Make sure you use plenty of it in your own life and business.

* What? You don't own it yet? Hurry! Get your copy of **You Are a Circle**, *before* they stop making books! :)

If you know you're not living at the fullest capacity, ask yourself: "Why not? . . . Why not?"

Be ruthless with any thought that attempts to rationalize your (or your business) limitations. No matter what kind of logical explanation you hear from within, or from without, keep asking, "Why not? . . ."

If you're bold enough to actually keep asking this question, you will find out that what separates your current position and the greatness you could achieve are just a set of actions you need to take, every day. These are your steps. For some, it might be perfecting their project; for others it might be learning a new skill.

As the popular adage says: "What kind a person (or brand) do you need to become in order to achieve the level of success you want?" Simply reverse-engineer it. Start from the end result and go backward. Chunk it down into small steps until you arrive at where you are today.

For how long should you take these steps?
Try every day, for the rest of your life.
It never ends. It's a process.
That's why growth is so interesting, in both life *and* business.

Experiment with something new. All the time. Just change one thing that could have a impact, and try making it a routine. It could be anything in your life or your business.

Right now, it's the end of the day and I'm going for a walk. Why? It keeps me healthy, and that's how I get my best ideas. I'm in pretty good shape today, but it hasn't always been this way. Action create change. So simply start with one decision. Right now. To improve anything in your life or your business, conduct hundreds of tiny experiments.

It's fun to see results manifesting from your efforts.

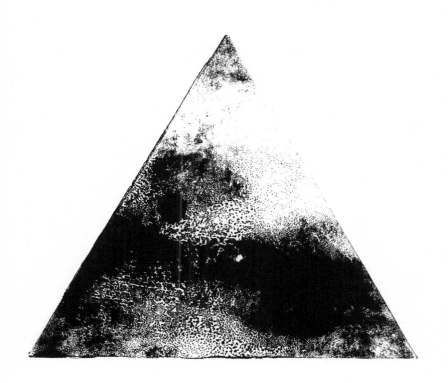

Even if you successfully work for clients, make sure you also create one little business on the side. Having your own project will keep you sane. Plus, you will learn a lot.

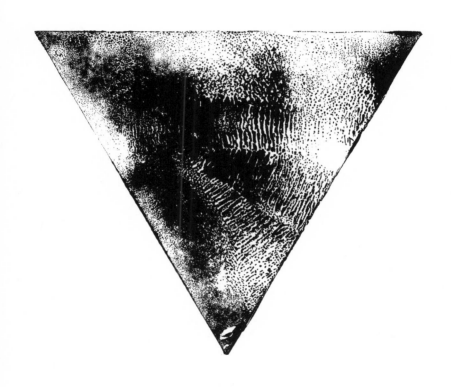

Being able to choose the right clients is a critical skill.

They should either have a cool factor so they can help you grow your brand awareness in your market, or they should bring good income.

The worst clients are the ones who don't pay well and have no cool factor to offer. Avoid them like the plague.

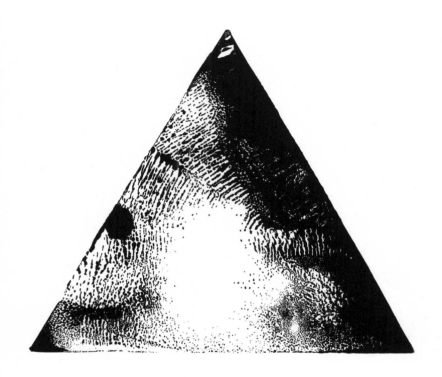

INFINITY   MIND   LIFE   HISTORY

CYBERNETICS   SCIENCE

                      PROCESSES

HOPE   EMOTIONS

    CONSCIOUSNESS   HEROES

LONG-TERM   CHALLENGE   SHIFT

       LOVE   PROGRESS

         HOME

EXPERIENCE   COMMUNICATION

SUSTAINABILITY   BIOLOGY

      COMMUNITY   PARTNERSHIPS

CHANGE

            EXPLORE

LEGACY   YOUR BRAND

           ENTHUSIASM

Connect the dots.   TRUTH   GROWTH

     YOU   VISION   PATTERNS

ART   UNKNOWN

   IDEAS   YOUTH   FUTURE

          TEAM

CULTURE   REVOLUTION

   DESIRE   EVOLUTION   HEART

PASSION

   ARCHETYPES TRINARY BLACK SWAN

WEALTH   MARKETS

  WHOLE   NEW

CREATE

        SALES

   WORK

      STORYTELLING MONEY

MAVERICK   MASTERY

TRENDS   EXPERIMENTS LIVING SYSTEMS

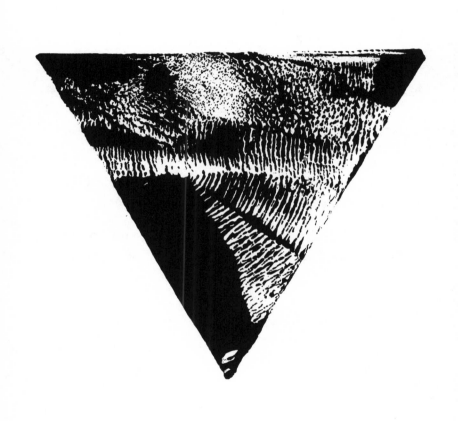

Preparation *and* selection is time management.

Time management is not as hard as you imagine. One simple habit is to write down your tasks, erasing them as you go. And at the end of the day, you simply build your list for the next day, adding the elements you missed at the top of your list.

In the same way, you can prepare your clothes the night before. Same thing with your breakfast, etc. When you wake up, everything is ready. You know what to do. It's go time.

Another classic strategy is to select your task by learning to prioritize. Simply ask yourself: "What's the value of this?" and act (or not) accordingly.

Sometimes, life can be hectic. Having rituals that support your physical and mental health is key, especially in the morning and evening.

I like to exercise right after I wake up. Before I go to bed, I meditate using specific soundscapes* I designed. Throughout the day, I also listen to music that helps me clear my mind; or I simply get infused by the specific energy of a song. It helps me refocus and connect with life in a different way. Everything in life has its own rhythm.

No matter what your rituals are, they're here to help you stay on track and see the big picture. They also support you through the hardest moments. That's the power of habits: Once they're in place, they force you to go where you need to go.

What are your everyday rituals?

*Download a free, meditative soundscape by visiting GuillaumeWolf.com and clicking on "Free Downloads."

Can you predict the future? No!

Future forecasting is tricky. Everyone in business is looking for an edge by making sure they don't miss out on "the next big thing." This demand creates a market for business seers who claim they can predict the future. Yet while this looks like a great idea (in theory), no one can ever get it right.*

No one can predict the future for a simple reason: <u>Change is nonlinear. Change is driven by living systems that elude analysis and forecasting.</u>

The only thing you can do in your business is to refine your approach every day by infusing it with innovations (or what I call experiments). This simple practice will make you stand out in your market, while avoiding the traps of trying to catch "the latest trend" that goes nowhere.

Creating a meaningful future starts with creating a solid present driven by the desire to innovate. The future is not hidden somewhere in a forecast, or in a trend blog; it starts with you and your creativity.

*To get a sense of the difficulty of predicting the future, read *Future Shock* by futurist Alvin Toffler. The book is an attempt to describe the world we live in today from the perspective of the seventies. Although he was the most respected futurist of his generation, Toffler's book is full of outrageous predictions that never panned out.

Can you predict the future? Yes!

Here's a paradox, while you can't predict the future by looking at trends, there are real visionaries out there who can sometimes get an accurate glimpse of the things to come.

One striking example is the case of Pierre Teilhard de Chardin, a French philosopher and Jesuit priest (his writings were censored by the Catholic Church). In his masterpiece, *The Phenomenon of Man*, he's able to combine his spiritual views with evolution into a functioning theory (an achievement in itself). Written in 1938, the book also predicts the coming of what Teilhard de Chardin calls a "Noosphere," which looks exactly like the Internet we know today. But there's more—he goes on to suggest that the presence of this web of information will accelerate the evolution of man—a major shift.

This book is extremely daring, and it's not an easy read. It's also a reflection of the author's beliefs and background. But it's so revolutionary and so accurate in many ways that it's worth reflecting upon. New ideas are never easy to understand at first—that's why they're new.

Are we on the verge of an evolutionary shift as Teilhard de Chardin offers? I don't know. But what I do know is that change is always embedded in the fabric of life. It always exists, right in front of us (even if we can't see it).

<u>Life is change. We are change. We are changing.</u>

A great way to get inspired creatively is to explore the world of daring visionaries. Try reading *The Phenomenon of Man*. It will make you think and wonder.

When you talk with top creatives, the world-class, they all mention stamina, the physicality of their job. Why? Because when you become really successful, your life completely changes as demands increase dramatically.

During an interview, designer extraordinaire Philippe Starck* once shared his calendar with me: It was insane. For several months, he was constantly flying off to a new destination, a new city, every day or so. "It *is* a monastic life," he confessed.

This is not uncommon. It's the same deal for everyone. One CEO I know travels so much, to avoid jet lag, he stays in the same time zone wherever he goes, booking meetings at 1:00 a.m. local time, if needed.

The secret is to treat your body as if you were a champion: You need to eat well. You need to exercise. You need to relax. You need to prepare yourself for the shock of hard work.

Extreme work dedication calls for extreme care.

When it comes to mind-body, what are the strategies you currently have in place to rejuvenate yourself?
What are the new ones you'd like to add?

Whitewall Magazine, issue 16.

Inspiration is paramount.
Inspiration comes from the love of culture.

If you really want to be great in your category, you need
to know about the culture you're in. All the best fashion
designers in the world know about the history of fashion.
All the best graphic designers in the world know about the
history of graphic design, etc. And as a common pattern, the
best creatives also always have extensive personal libraries
and archives.

Why books versus online research? Because there are
a lot of books that are *not* online. When you have access to the
right references, you have an edge.

No one ever creates anything out of thin air. No matter
what business you're in, it always lives within a specific cultural context. If you don't know about the culture you're a part
of, you have no lasting power.

How many books do you have about the culture you're in?
How many books do you buy each month?

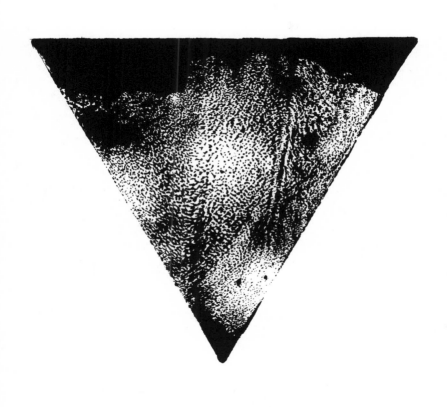

Many cultures believe in predestination, meaning the absence of free will. Some call it "the will of God," some call it "karma."

Yet when you're in business, you become a creator, and in essence, you *have* to believe in free will.

But . . .

I found out through life experience (because I'm old enough) that, perhaps, life may work with these two principles simultaenously. Maybe we *are* predestined, and within that space, we also have the complete freedom to create our best (or worst) possible self. Predestined, yet co-creators.

Once you get that you can only live your *own* life (versus someone else's), you also come to the realization that you will *never* be like this Olympic athlete or this opera signer (who were born for the job). This doesn't mean you can't dream big. Quite the opposite, actually. Because now, it becomes interesting, you have to ask yourself: "What was I born to do?"

When you find the answer to that riddle and you create your life (and business) around it, everything changes.

Keep asking:

> What makes you unique?
> What were you born to do?

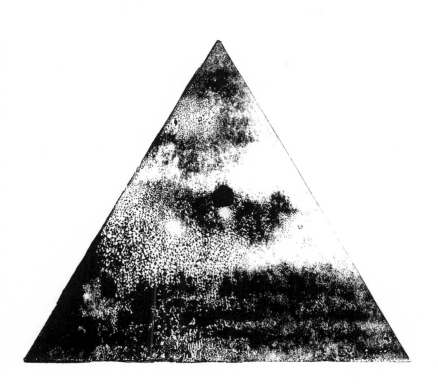

There's a strange, almost spiritual side to business (and life). After years of practice, it gets really interesting because you move into abstraction. The more you progress, the more you realize you've devised your own game, so to speak. And every day, you have to keep growing within it.

You're in it to perfect your gesture.

You're in it to practice purposeful action.

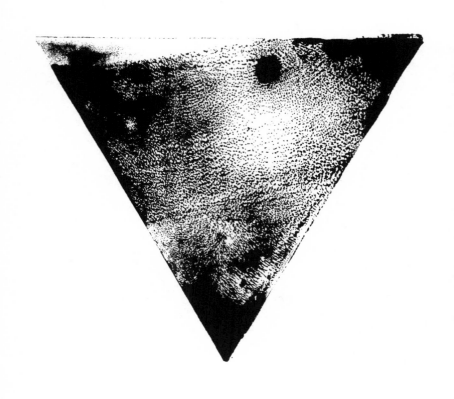

You are appreciated the most when you let your true self shine. The same thing with your brand.

Meditate on this one.

You need to create for yourself a definition of success that's bulletproof to the downturns life will throw at you.

Most people think about success in terms of monetary gains—which is just a part of it. But there's more.

What happens when you lose everything due to events over which you have no control? Are you now becoming a failure? Is your life over?

Of course not.

Success is a mental process. It's a journey through ups and down, driven by continuous improvements, persistence, long-term vision, truth, focus, and hard work.

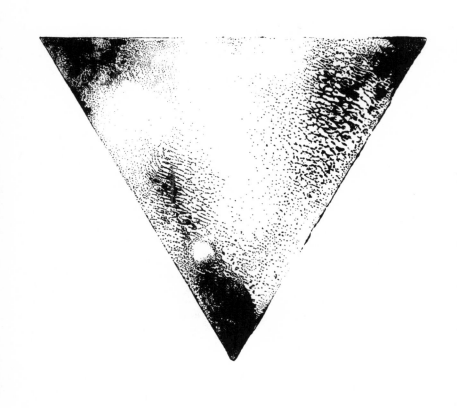

I can claim with full confidence and absolute authority that I'm the most idiotic person I know. I've made all the mistakes that can be made. I am an official World-Class-Champion-at-Making-Mistakes™.

But I'm also persistent. I never quit. And every time, I learn something new. Then, I always try again with a different approach until something works. I thrive on experimenting, learning, and refining.

I'm not a genius at anything—I really wish I were smarter. But every day, I keep trying until positive results show up. And they always do.

Try it too: *Try to try!* It seems to be working.

Try, try, try, and try again.

When we're ready to wake up for a moment, work hard together, and tap into our creative mind, we're going to change the world for the better. We can all be a part of this movement.

Everyone is invited.
And that includes *you*, my friend.

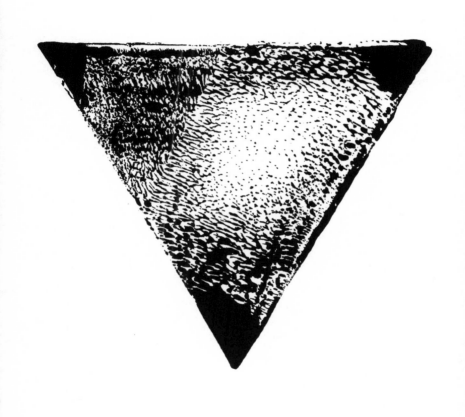

It all starts with an idea. It all starts with a vision. It all starts with you saying, "Why not? I'm going to try this."

No matter where you are right now, life is waiting for you to act. She wants you to create something good. Something life-affirming. She wants to be surprised by your dedication.

Show her what you've got.

Yes, she's a tough audience, and yes, she will hit you hard, because she wants to see real effort coming from you. She wants to see nothing less than your absolute best.

So, it's going to be hard, and that's good.

Because when you perform well, she will reward you beyond your imagination. She will reward you with growth, adventure, satisfaction, meaning, belonging, and the newfound joy of simply being yourself. She will reward you with this elusive gift called "happiness."

So now, you know what to do:

Say, "Why not?" . . . and **go for it**.

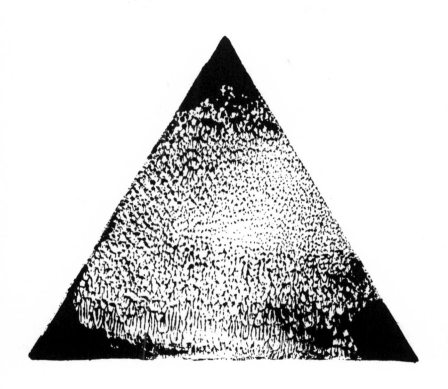

Tabula rasa
(Blank slate)

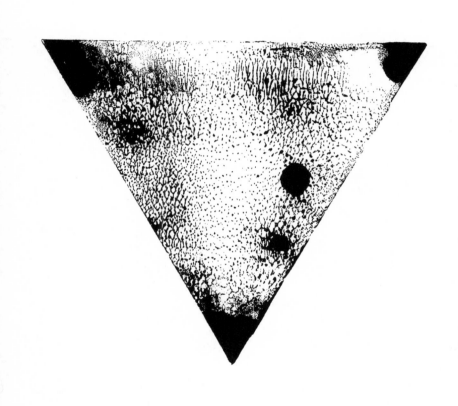

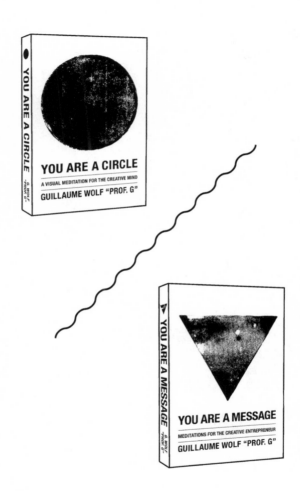

A MESSAGE FROM GUILLAUME

Hello, creative friend,

I hope you've enjoyed exploring this concept book and that it will inspire you to go out there and do great things.

This book and its companion, **You Are a Circle**, are part of the little experiments I've talked about in this volume.

<u>What you have in your hands *is* an experiment in publishing:</u> It's inspiration, learning, and art combined. It was done alone: self-published and self-promoted.

Today many professionals still believe self-publishing is impossible. And my goal is to see if, *<u>together, we can make the impossible become real.</u>* These experiments can only work if <u>we partner together as a team.</u> In that sense, this book is symbiotic: It belongs to **you**.

I write *and* illustrate these books on my free time. I'm a teacher and a dad, and I also have a design/consulting practice; but every day, I work extra hard to create projects to inspire other creatives. So if you really like this book and want to see more in the future, please join in and support it.

<u>What you can do:</u> Simply post about this book on your social media platform: Use **#youareamessage** and **#youareacircle**. And, if you're inclined, feel free to leave a review on Amazon.com—it really helps, and it's super-nice to hear from you.

I really appreciate your support.

Thank you
Guillaume "Prof. G"

ABOUT THE AUTHOR

An author, teacher, consultant, and visual artist, Guillaume Wolf is a branding and communication expert.

Wolf trained as a designer and communicator. He is known for his acclaimed creative direction work for fashion and luxury brands. In his private consulting and design practice, he advises brands and organizations on brand ideation, creation, identity, and communication.

A preeminent expert in applied psychographics, Wolf is a full-time faculty member at Art Center College of Design in Pasadena, California, where he teaches communication design and the psychology behind branding.

Wolf is the author of several books on creativity, including the indie hit concept book, *You Are a Circle*.

www.ProfG.co

MORE?

Are you curious to discover more?

For workshop information, and complimentary content, please visit: **www.ProfG.co**

Made in the USA
San Bernardino, CA
22 May 2017